TUBA

AUDIO ACCESS INCLUDED

PLAYBACK+
lance • Loop

EASY Improvisation

T0085506

2 How to Use This Book

3 Bossa Nova
4 Calypso
5 Cinematic
6 Cha-Cha Major
7 Cha-Cha Minor
8 Country Blues
9 Country Waltz
10 Cumbia
11 Disco
12 Drumline
13 E.D.M.
14 '50s Slow Rock
15 Funk
16 Gypsy Flamenco
17 Heavy Metal

18 Hip-Hop
19 Jazz Dominant 7th
20 Jazz Dorian 1
21 Jazz Dorian 2
22 Jazz Major
23 Liverpool
24 Mambo
25 Middle Eastern
26 Piano Ballad
27 Pirates
28 R&B
29 Reggae
30 Rock 'n' Roll
31 '60s Folk
32 Zydeco

To access audio visit:
www.halleonard.com/mylibrary

Enter Code
4171-1697-8966-6515

Audio Arrangements and Music by Peter Deneff

ISBN 978-1-4950-9652-5

HAL•LEONARD®

7777 W. BLUEMOUND RD. P.O. BOX 13819 MILWAUKEE, WI 53213

In Australia Contact:
Hal Leonard Australia Pty. Ltd.
4 Lentara Court
Cheltenham, Victoria, 3192 Australia
Email: ausadmin@halleonard.com.au

Visit Hal Leonard Online at
www.halleonard.com

HOW TO USE THIS BOOK

Introduction

Easy Improvisation is an introduction to improvisation for any student in the band. It can be used by

- an individual player, to be played with the *PLAYBACK+* audio
- a small group of players, to be played with or without the *PLAYBACK+* audio
- a large ensemble, to be played with or without the *PLAYBACK+* audio

When learning to improvise, often a challenge is that the musician is given too much freedom. "Just play what you feel" does little good, and is the opposite of what most players have been told from the beginning: to play what's on the page. *Easy Improvisation* includes suggested notes to be used while improvising, and even four sample solos, using these notes.

How to Play Each Exercise

- The first three staves are meant to be the background, repeated as you would like throughout. In a larger group setting, these can be played by some musicians, while others improvise.
- The shorter staff in the middle of the page is a scale, upon which you can base your improvisation.
- There are then four solos written out, using the notes from the scale. You can play one (or more) of these solos, or make up your own!

"When improvising, what do I play?"

Use the sample notes given. First just use one note, with simple changes to the rhythm. Then, as you feel more comfortable, use two notes, then three, and so on. You will hear what notes sound better than others, and stick with those. Improvisation does not need to be fast playing. The more you practice improvising, the more comfortable you will become with it.

How to Use the *PLAYBACK+* Audio

To access the accompaniment and demo tracks, visit www.halleonard.com/mylibrary and enter the 16-digit code found on the previous page. Each exercise is a 4-measure phrase, repeated 16 times (64 measures total). The demo track includes rhythm instruments, chord changes, and all the notes on the page.

This is how the demo track is laid out:

- Two measures of click track count off.
- The first three lines are played, with each new line layered on top of each other. After the third line is played, all three lines are played together again.
- Each solo is played one at a time, alternating with the accompaniment only.
- Then the "head" returns, with the first three lines layered on top of each other. After the third line is played, all three lines are played together again.
- A final chord brings the music to a close.

During the solo section, students are encouraged to "call and respond" or "trade 4's" with the sample solos. Or, for a more extended solo, use the accompaniment track. The accompaniment track is also 64 measures long, but has no melodic instruments playing.

Above all, we hope *Easy Improvisation* can guide you as you become more comfortable with improvisation. Have fun!

BOSSA NOVA

TUBA

Use the following major scale for improvisation.

CALYPSO

TUBA

Use the following major scale for improvisation.

CINEMATIC

TUBA

Slowly, mysteriously

Use the following minor scale for improvisation.

Solo 1

Solo 2

Solo 3

Solo 4

CHA-CHA MAJOR

TUBA

Use the following major scale for improvisation.

CHA-CHA MINOR

TUBA

Use the following harmonic minor scale for improvisation.

Or, you could use the following melodic minor scale.

COUNTRY BLUES

TUBA

Use the following modified major blues scale for improvisation.

Solo 1

Solo 2

Solo 3

Solo 4

COUNTRY WALTZ

TUBA

Use the following major scale for improvisation.

Solo 1

Solo 2

Solo 3

Solo 4

CUMBIA

TUBA

Use the following Mixolydian scale for improvisation.

Solo 1

Solo 2

Solo 3

Solo 4

DISCO

TUBA

Use following Dorian scale for improvisation.

Solo 1

Solo 2

Solo 3

Solo 4

DRUMLINE

TUBA

Use the following major scale for improvisation.

E.D.M.

TUBA

Use the following minor scale for improvisation.

'50S SLOW ROCK

TUBA

Use the following major scale for improvisation.

Solo 1

Solo 2

Solo 3

Solo 4

FUNK

TUBA

Use the following Dorian scale for improvisation.

GYPSY FLAMENCO

TUBA

Use the following Phrygian scale for improvisation.

(use with D)

HEAVY METAL

TUBA

Use the following Dorian scale for improvisation.

Solo 1

Solo 2

Solo 3

Solo 4

HIP-HOP

TUBA

Use the following Dorian scale for improvisation.

Solo 1

Solo 2

Solo 3

Solo 4

JAZZ DOMINANT 7TH

TUBA

Use the following modified major blues scale for improvisation.

JAZZ DORIAN 1

TUBA

Moderately

Use the following Dorian scale for improvisation.

Solo 1

Solo 2

Solo 3

Solo 4

JAZZ DORIAN 2

TUBA

Use the following Dorian scale for improvisation.

Solo 1

Solo 2

Solo 3

Solo 4

JAZZ MAJOR

TUBA

Use the following major scale for improvisation.

LIVERPOOL

TUBA

Use the following minor blues scale for improvisation.

Solo 1

Solo 2

Solo 3

Solo 4

MAMBO

TUBA

Use the following Mixolydian scale for improvisation.

Solo 1

Solo 2

Solo 3

Solo 4

MIDDLE EASTERN

Use the following Phrygian scale for improvisation.

PIANO BALLAD

TUBA

Use the following major scale for improvisation.

Solo 1

Solo 2

Solo 3

Solo 4

PIRATES

TUBA

Use the following minor scale for improvisation.

R&B

TUBA

Use the following modified major blues scale for improvisation.

REGGAE

TUBA

Moderately

Use the followin Dorian scale for improvisation.

Or, you could use the following minor blues scale.

Solo 1

Solo 2

Solo 3

Solo 4

ROCK 'N' ROLL

TUBA

Use the following blues scale for improvisation.

Solo 1

Solo 2

Solo 3

Solo 4

'60S FOLK

TUBA

Use the following major scale for improvisation.

ZYDECO

TUBA

Use the following blues scale for improvisation.

Solo 1

Solo 2

Solo 3

Solo 4